Mindful Balance: Attaining Inner Peace in the Modern World

SALMAN KHAN

Mindful Balance: Attaining Inner Peace in the Modern World
Copyright © 2023 by SALMAN KHAN

All rights reserved. No part of this book may be reproduced or transmitted in any form or by any means, electronic or mechanical, including photocopying, recording, or by any information storage and retrieval system, without permission in writing from the publisher.

This book is a work of fiction. Names, characters, places, and incidents either are the product of the author's imagination or are used fictitiously. Any resemblance to actual events, locales, persons, living or dead, is entirely coincidental.

The first edition was published in 2023

ISBN:

Published by:
Noya
1663 Liberty Drive
Hyderabad, IN 47403
www.noyapublishers.com

This book is self-published using on-demand printing and publishing, which allows it to be printed and distributed globally.

TABLE OF CONTENTS

Chapter 1: Understanding Inner Peace in the Modern World — 07
The Concept of Inner Peace

Challenges in Attaining Inner Peace in the Modern World

Chapter 2: Importance of Balancing Work and Life — 11
The Impact of Work-Life Imbalance on Inner Peace

Benefits of Achieving Work-Life Balance

Chapter 3: Assessing Your Work-Life Balance — 15
Identifying Areas of Imbalance

Self-Reflection and Evaluation Techniques

Chapter 4: Strategies for Balancing Work and Life — 19
Setting Priorities and Boundaries

Time Management Techniques for Achieving Balance

Delegating and Outsourcing to Reduce Workload

Chapter 5: Mindfulness Practices for Inner Peace 25

Introduction to Mindfulness

Mindful Breathing and Meditation Techniques

Incorporating Mindfulness into Daily Life

Chapter 6: Developing Self-Care Habits 31

Importance of Self-Care for Inner Peace

Physical Self-Care Practices

Emotional and Mental Self-Care Practices

Chapter 7: Nurturing Relationships for Inner Peace 37

Balancing Personal and Professional Relationships

Effective Communication for Harmonious Relationships

Cultivating Empathy and Compassion in Relationships

Chapter 8: Embracing Minimalism and Simplifying Your Life 43

Understanding the Benefits of Minimalism

Decluttering and Organizing Your Physical Space

Simplifying Your Digital Life

Chapter 9: Overcoming Stress and Anxiety　　　49

Identifying Sources of Stress and Anxiety

Stress Management Techniques

Coping Strategies for Dealing with Anxiety

Chapter 10: Maintaining Balance in a Fast-Paced World　　　55

Strategies for Staying Grounded Amidst Chaos

Creating a Sustainable Routine for Inner Peace

Embracing Flexibility and Adaptability

Chapter 11: Sustaining Inner Peace for Long-term Happiness　　　61

Cultivating Gratitude and Positive Thinking

Self-Reflection and Continuous Growth

Building a Supportive Community for Lasting Inner Peace

Conclusion: Embracing Mindful Balance in the Modern World　　　67

Chapter 1: Understanding Inner Peace in the Modern World

The Concept of Inner Peace

In today's fast-paced and demanding world, finding inner peace seems like an elusive goal. We are constantly juggling multiple responsibilities, striving for success, and trying to keep up with the ever-increasing demands of our personal and professional lives. However, amidst this chaos, there exists a concept that can bring solace and tranquility into our lives – the concept of inner peace.

Inner peace is not just a state of mind; it is a way of life. It is the ability to maintain a sense of calm and harmony within ourselves, regardless of external circumstances. It is about finding a balance between our work and personal life, and nurturing our mental, emotional, and spiritual well-being.

In the modern world, where the lines between work and life are often blurred, achieving inner peace becomes even more crucial. Balancing work and life is essential for our overall well-being and happiness. When we are constantly overwhelmed by the demands of work, it can take a toll on our mental and physical health, leading to stress, anxiety, and burnout. On the other hand, neglecting our work responsibilities can lead to feelings of guilt and dissatisfaction.

To achieve inner peace, we need to create a mindful balance between our work and life. This involves setting clear boundaries, prioritizing self-care, and cultivating healthy habits. It means learning to say no when necessary, delegating tasks, and seeking support when needed. It also means making time for activities that bring us joy and nourish our soul, such as spending time with loved ones, pursuing hobbies, or simply taking a moment to connect with nature.

Finding inner peace also requires a deep understanding of ourselves and our values. It involves exploring our beliefs, desires, and fears, and aligning our actions with our truest selves. It means letting go of attachments and expectations and embracing the present moment fully. Inner peace is not about achieving a state of perpetual happiness; it is about accepting the inevitable ups and downs of life with grace and equanimity.

conclusion,

inner peace is not an unattainable goal reserved for a select few; it is a concept that can be embraced by all types of individuals. It is about finding harmony within ourselves and nurturing our well-being. By cultivating a mindful balance between work and life, and by deepening our understanding of ourselves, we can embark on a journey towards inner peace in the modern world.

Challenges in Attaining Inner Peace in the Modern World

In today's fast-paced and demanding world, finding inner peace can be a daunting task. The constant juggling act of balancing work and life can leave us feeling overwhelmed, stressed, and disconnected from ourselves. This subchapter aims to explore the challenges that we encounter, as well as provide insights and practical tips to help you attain inner peace amidst the chaos.

One of the primary challenges in attaining inner peace is the ever-increasing pressure to excel in both our personal and professional lives. The pursuit of success often comes at the cost of our mental and emotional well-being. We find ourselves caught up in a never-ending cycle of busyness, constantly striving for more, and neglecting our inner needs. This constant striving can leave us feeling empty and disconnected from our true selves.

Another challenge is the technological revolution that has brought convenience but also unleashed a host of distractions. We are constantly bombarded with notifications, emails, and social media updates, leaving us with little time to quiet our minds and find inner stillness. The addictive nature of technology can make it difficult to detach and be present in the moment, hindering our ability to attain inner peace.

Additionally, the blurred boundaries between work and personal life pose a significant challenge to achieving inner peace. The pressures of a competitive work environment can spill into our personal lives, causing us to sacrifice our well-being for the sake of professional success. It becomes crucial to establish healthy boundaries and prioritize self-care to prevent burnout and maintain a sense of balance.

However, amidst these challenges, attaining inner peace is not impossible. By incorporating mindfulness practices into our daily routines, we can cultivate a sense of calm and balance. Engaging in activities such as meditation, yoga, or simply spending quality time in nature can help us reconnect with ourselves and find inner stillness.

Furthermore, setting realistic expectations and learning to say no are essential in finding balance. Understanding that we cannot do it all and that it is okay to prioritize our well-being is crucial in attaining inner peace. By creating a harmonious work-life integration, we can reduce stress and find more fulfillment in both areas.

conclusion,

the modern world presents us with numerous challenges in our pursuit of inner peace. However, by recognizing these challenges and implementing mindful practices, we can navigate through the chaos and find the balance we seek. Remember, inner peace is not a destination but rather a journey, and it is within our reach, regardless of our circumstances.

Chapter 2: Importance of Balancing Work and Life

The Impact of Work-Life Imbalance on Inner Peace

In today's fast-paced and demanding world, achieving a sense of inner peace seems like an elusive goal for many. One of the major factors contributing to this struggle is work-life imbalance. The constant juggling between professional responsibilities and personal obligations takes a toll on our overall well-being and hinders our ability to find inner peace.

Work-life imbalance can manifest in various ways, such as spending excessive hours at work, neglecting personal relationships, sacrificing hobbies and interests, and failing to prioritize self-care. The consequences of this imbalance ripple through our lives, affecting our mental, emotional, and physical health.

One of the most significant impacts of work-life imbalance on our inner peace is heightened stress levels. When work takes precedence over personal life, stress becomes a constant companion. The pressure to meet deadlines, achieve targets, and excel in our careers can lead to burnout and chronic stress, leaving us feeling overwhelmed and disconnected from ourselves.

Moreover, work-life imbalance often leads to strained relationships. Neglecting our loved ones can result in feelings of guilt, resentment, and loneliness. These negative emotions further erode our inner peace, as we find ourselves torn between professional success and nurturing meaningful connections.

Additionally, when work dominates our lives, we tend to neglect our physical well-being. Lack of exercise, disrupted sleep patterns, and poor eating habits can lead to various health issues, including fatigue, obesity, and even chronic diseases. Such physical ailments not only impact our overall well-being but also disrupt our inner peace, as our bodies and minds are intrinsically connected.

To regain our inner peace, it is crucial to address work-life imbalance and strive for a better equilibrium. Creating boundaries between work and personal life, setting realistic expectations, and making time for self-care are essential steps towards restoring balance. Taking regular breaks, engaging in activities that bring joy, and nurturing relationships can help us reconnect with ourselves and find solace amidst life's challenges.

In the book "Mindful Balance: Attaining Inner Peace in the Modern World," we delve deeper into the intricacies of work-life imbalance and provide practical strategies to achieve harmony. Whether you are a busy professional, a stay-at-home parent, or someone struggling to find a balance, this subchapter is designed to help you navigate the complexities of modern life and cultivate inner peace.

Remember, achieving inner peace is not a destination but a journey. By addressing work-life imbalance and prioritizing self-care, we can gradually create a life that nourishes our souls and brings us closer to lasting inner peace.

Benefits of Achieving Work-Life Balance

In today's fast-paced world, achieving a harmonious work-life balance has become increasingly challenging. Many individuals find themselves constantly juggling between demanding work responsibilities and personal commitments, leaving little time for self-care and relaxation. However, it is crucial to acknowledge that achieving work-life balance is not just a luxury; it is essential for our overall well-being and inner peace.

One of the primary benefits of attaining work-life balance is reduced stress levels. When we are overwhelmed with work and neglect our personal lives, stress builds up, leading to physical and mental health issues. By allocating time for both work and personal activities, we can experience reduced stress, improved sleep quality, and enhanced overall health. This, in turn, allows us to approach our professional and personal lives with renewed energy and focus.

Another advantage of work-life balance is increased productivity and efficiency. When we constantly push ourselves to work long hours without taking breaks, our performance tends to suffer. By incorporating regular breaks, exercise, and leisure activities into our routine, we can refresh our minds and increase our productivity. Studies have shown that individuals who prioritize work-life balance tend to be more engaged, creative, and innovative in their work, leading to better job satisfaction and career growth.

Achieving work-life balance also strengthens our relationships and promotes personal growth. When we find time for our families, friends, and hobbies, we create deeper connections and foster a sense of belonging. Nurturing these relationships not only brings joy and fulfillment but also provides a support system during challenging times. Moreover, dedicating time for personal growth activities such as learning new skills or pursuing hobbies allows us to explore our passions and interests, leading to a more fulfilling and purposeful life.

Lastly, work-life balance promotes self-care and self-reflection. Taking care of our physical, emotional, and mental well-being is crucial for maintaining inner peace. By prioritizing self-care activities such as exercise, meditation, or spending time in nature, we can recharge ourselves and cultivate a sense of mindfulness. This allows us to gain clarity, identify our values and priorities, and align our actions accordingly, leading to a more fulfilling and balanced life.

conclusion,

achieving work-life balance is not just an aspiration; it is a necessity for our overall well-being and inner peace. By reducing stress, increasing productivity, strengthening relationships, and promoting self-care, work-life balance empowers us to lead healthier, more fulfilling lives. It is essential for individuals of all types, regardless of their profession or personal circumstances, to prioritize the cultivation of work-life balance and attain inner peace in the modern world.

Chapter 3: Assessing Your Work-Life Balance

Identifying Areas of Imbalance

In our fast-paced and demanding modern world, finding inner peace can often feel like an elusive goal. We are constantly bombarded with responsibilities, deadlines, and expectations, leaving little time for self-reflection and self-care. However, achieving a mindful balance is not only possible but essential to our overall well-being.

In this subchapter, we will explore the importance of identifying areas of imbalance in our lives and how to restore harmony between work and personal life. This is a topic that resonates with all types of individuals, regardless of their background or profession. Whether you are a busy executive, a dedicated parent, or someone struggling to find purpose and meaning, the principles discussed here will help you regain control and attain inner peace.

The first step towards finding balance is self-awareness. Take a moment to assess your current situation and honestly evaluate where you feel out of sync. Are you spending an excessive amount of time at work, neglecting your personal life and relationships? Or do you find yourself constantly distracted by personal matters while at work, hindering your productivity?

Once you have identified the areas of imbalance, it is important to prioritize and set boundaries. Balancing work and life requires making conscious choices about how you spend your time and energy. Consider what truly matters to you and allocate your resources accordingly. Learn to say no to commitments that do not align with your values or contribute positively to your overall well-being.

Another crucial aspect of attaining inner peace is self-care. It is easy to neglect our physical, emotional, and mental health when we are caught up in the daily grind. However, taking care of ourselves is not a luxury but a necessity. Make time for activities that rejuvenate and nourish your mind, body, and soul. Whether it's practicing mindfulness, engaging in physical exercise, or pursuing a hobby, these activities will help restore balance and enhance your overall sense of well-being.

Lastly, remember that achieving mindful balance is an ongoing process. It requires constant reflection, adjustment, and self-compassion. Be patient and kind to yourself as you navigate the challenges of balancing work and life. Embrace the journey and celebrate the small victories along the way.

In conclusion, identifying areas of imbalance is the first step towards attaining inner peace in the modern world. Regardless of your background or circumstances, finding balance between work and personal life is essential for your overall well-being. By becoming self-aware, setting boundaries, prioritizing self-care, and embracing the journey, you can create a harmonious and fulfilling life that brings you inner peace.

Self-Reflection and Evaluation Techniques

In our fast-paced modern world, finding inner peace can seem like an elusive goal. Balancing work and life can be a constant struggle, leaving us feeling overwhelmed and disconnected from ourselves. However, by implementing self-reflection and evaluation techniques, we can begin to attain the much-needed inner peace we all crave.

Self-reflection is the practice of looking inward and examining our thoughts, emotions, and actions. It allows us to gain a deeper understanding of ourselves and the impact we have on our own well-being. By taking the time to reflect on our lives, we can identify areas that need attention and make necessary changes to achieve a more balanced and peaceful existence.

One powerful self-reflection technique is journaling. By putting pen to paper, we can explore our thoughts and emotions in a safe and non-judgmental space. This process allows us to gain clarity, release pent-up emotions, and gain insight into our own patterns and behaviors. Regular journaling can be a cathartic and transformative practice that leads us to a greater sense of inner peace.

Another valuable technique is meditation. Meditation provides an opportunity to quiet the mind, focus on the present moment, and cultivate a sense of inner calm. By incorporating daily meditation into our routine, we can reduce stress, improve focus, and enhance overall well-being. Even just a few minutes of dedicated meditation each day can have significant benefits for our mental and emotional health.

In addition to self-reflection, evaluation techniques are essential in finding a balance between work and life. We often get caught up in the demands of our jobs and neglect other important aspects of our lives, such as relationships, hobbies, and self-care. By regularly evaluating our priorities and goals, we can ensure that we are dedicating time and energy to all areas that contribute to our inner peace.

One effective evaluation technique is creating a work-life balance wheel. This visual tool allows us to assess how much time and energy we are dedicating to different areas of our lives. By identifying areas that are lacking attention, we can make conscious efforts to rebalance and prioritize accordingly. This technique helps us make intentional choices and avoid burnout or neglecting important aspects of our lives.

In conclusion, self-reflection and evaluation techniques are powerful tools in achieving inner peace while balancing work and life. By taking the time to reflect on our thoughts and emotions, journaling, and incorporating meditation into our routines, we can gain insight into ourselves and cultivate a sense of calm. Additionally, evaluating our priorities and using tools such as the work-life balance wheel can ensure that we are dedicating time and energy to all areas that contribute to our overall well-being. By practicing these techniques regularly, we can attain the much-needed inner peace in our modern world.

Chapter 4: Strategies for Balancing Work and Life

Setting Priorities and Boundaries

In today's fast-paced and demanding world, finding inner peace can seem like an elusive goal. We often find ourselves juggling multiple responsibilities and struggling to strike a balance between work and personal life. However, the key to attaining inner peace lies in setting priorities and boundaries.

Prioritizing is the art of identifying what truly matters to us and aligning our actions accordingly. It involves understanding our values, goals, and aspirations, and making deliberate choices that reflect them. By setting clear priorities, we can focus our time and energy on what truly brings us joy and fulfillment, rather than getting caught up in the constant busyness and distractions of modern life.

To start prioritizing, it is essential to take a step back and evaluate our current commitments and obligations. We need to ask ourselves: Are these activities aligned with our values and goals? Do they contribute to our overall well-being and inner peace? By critically examining our commitments, we can identify areas where we may need to make adjustments or let go of certain responsibilities that no longer serve us.

Boundaries act as our personal guidelines for maintaining a healthy work-life balance. They help us create a sense of order and structure in our lives, preventing burnout and allowing us to prioritize self-care. Establishing boundaries means learning to say no when necessary and setting limits on our time and energy. It also involves creating designated spaces and times for work, leisure, and relaxation.

In today's hyper-connected world, technology often blurs the lines between work and personal life. It is crucial to set boundaries when it comes to our use of technology, such as turning off notifications during personal time and setting specific hours for work-related communication.

Setting priorities and boundaries requires courage and self-awareness. It may involve making difficult choices and confronting societal expectations or internal pressures. However, by aligning our actions with our values and creating healthy boundaries, we can experience a greater sense of inner peace and fulfillment.

Remember, finding balance is an ongoing process. It requires regular self-reflection and adjustment as our priorities and circumstances change. By consciously setting priorities and boundaries, we can create a harmonious and fulfilling life that nourishes our well-being and allows us to thrive in both our personal and professional spheres.

Time Management Techniques for Achieving Balance

In today's fast-paced and demanding world, finding the balance between work and personal life can be a real challenge. Many of us find ourselves constantly overwhelmed and struggling to keep up with the demands of our careers while still maintaining a fulfilling personal life. However, with the right time management techniques, it is possible to achieve a sense of balance and inner peace.

One of the most effective techniques for balancing work and life is prioritization. Often, we have a long list of tasks and responsibilities that need our attention. By identifying the most important and urgent tasks and focusing on them first, we can ensure that we are making progress in both our professional and personal lives. This can involve setting clear goals, creating to-do lists, and breaking tasks down into manageable chunks.

Another crucial aspect of time management is learning to say no. Many of us have a tendency to take on too much, whether it's at work or in our personal lives. It is important to recognize our limits and be selective about the commitments we take on. By saying no to certain tasks or activities that do not align with our priorities, we can free up more time and energy for the things that truly matter.

Additionally, setting boundaries is essential for achieving balance. This means establishing clear guidelines for when and how much time we dedicate to work and personal life. It can involve setting specific work hours and sticking to them, as well as carving out dedicated time for relaxation, hobbies, and spending quality time with loved ones. By creating these boundaries, we can prevent work from spilling over into our personal lives and vice versa.

Furthermore, effective time management involves utilizing technology and tools to our advantage. There are numerous apps, calendars, and productivity tools available that can help us stay organized, prioritize tasks, and manage our time more efficiently. By harnessing the power of technology, we can streamline our workflow and reduce stress.

conclusion,

achieving a balance between work and personal life is crucial for attaining inner peace in the modern world. By implementing these time management techniques such as prioritization, learning to say no, setting boundaries, and utilizing technology, we can create a more harmonious and fulfilling life. Remember, finding balance is a continuous process, and it requires regular evaluation and adjustment. With commitment and practice, we can achieve a mindful balance that allows us to thrive in both our professional and personal lives.

Delegating and Outsourcing to Reduce Workload

In today's fast-paced and demanding world, finding a balance between work and personal life has become increasingly challenging. The constant pressure to do more, be more productive, and meet multiple deadlines can leave us feeling overwhelmed and stressed. However, there is a way to attain inner peace amidst the chaos – by learning the art of delegating and outsourcing.

Delegating tasks is a powerful tool that allows us to lighten our workload and create more time for ourselves. It involves entrusting specific responsibilities to others who are capable and willing to assist us. Whether you are a busy professional, a stay-at-home parent, or a student, delegating tasks can help you regain control of your life and find that much-needed balance.

One of the key benefits of delegating is the reduction of stress. By sharing the workload with others, you can focus on the tasks that truly require your attention and expertise. This not only eases the burden on your shoulders but also allows you to achieve better results in a shorter time. Additionally, delegating empowers those around you, providing them with an opportunity to grow and develop their skills.

Outsourcing is another strategy that can significantly contribute to reducing your workload. It involves hiring external professionals or services to handle specific tasks that are outside your area of expertise or consume excessive time. For example, you can outsource administrative tasks, social media management, or even household chores. By doing so, you can free up your time and energy for activities that bring you joy and fulfillment.

However, it is important to approach delegating and outsourcing mindfully. Start by identifying tasks that can be effectively delegated or outsourced without compromising quality. Clearly communicate your expectations and provide necessary guidelines to ensure a smooth workflow. Trust the abilities of those you delegate to and give them the freedom to excel in their assigned tasks.

Remember, delegating and outsourcing are not signs of weakness or incompetence; rather, they are strategies to optimize your time and energy. By practicing these techniques, you can create a harmonious balance between work and life, leading to inner peace and a greater sense of fulfillment.

conclusion,

finding inner peace in the modern world requires us to take control of our workload and find a balance between work and personal life. Delegating and outsourcing are powerful tools that can help us achieve this balance. By entrusting tasks to others and hiring external help, we can reduce our workload, alleviate stress, and create more time for ourselves. Remember to approach these strategies mindfully, clearly communicate expectations, and trust in the abilities of those you delegate to. Through delegating and outsourcing, we can attain the mindful balance we seek, leading to inner peace and a more fulfilling life.

Chapter 5: Mindfulness Practices for Inner Peace

Introduction to Mindfulness

In today's fast-paced and chaotic world, finding inner peace and balance seems like an elusive dream. The constant demands of work and personal life can leave us feeling overwhelmed, stressed, and disconnected from ourselves. However, there is a powerful tool that can help us regain control and achieve harmony - mindfulness.

Mindfulness is a practice with ancient roots that has gained significant popularity in recent years. It involves paying attention to the present moment and cultivating a non-judgmental awareness of our thoughts, feelings, and sensations. By doing so, we can learn to navigate the ups and downs of life with grace and find inner peace amidst the chaos.

This subchapter, "Introduction to Mindfulness," aims to provide a comprehensive understanding of mindfulness and how it can be applied to balance work and life for inner peace. Whether you are a busy professional, a homemaker, a student, or anyone seeking a sense of equilibrium, this chapter is designed to be accessible and relevant to all types of individuals.

We will begin by exploring the origins of mindfulness, tracing its roots back to ancient wisdom traditions such as Buddhism. By understanding its historical and philosophical background, we can grasp the essence of mindfulness and its significance in the modern world.

Next, we will delve into the science behind mindfulness. Numerous studies have shown that practicing mindfulness can have a profound impact on our well-being, reducing stress, anxiety, and depression while enhancing focus, creativity, and overall emotional resilience. We will explore the research findings and discuss how mindfulness can benefit our personal and professional lives.

Furthermore, we will provide practical guidance on how to incorporate mindfulness into our daily routines. From simple breathing exercises to formal meditation practices, we will offer a variety of techniques that can be tailored to fit different lifestyles and schedules. By integrating mindfulness into our lives, we can cultivate a deeper sense of presence and awareness, leading to greater clarity, productivity, and overall happiness.

Ultimately, the goal of this subchapter is to empower you with the knowledge and tools to embark on your mindfulness journey. By embracing mindfulness, you can find the balance you seek, creating a harmonious and fulfilling life in the midst of the modern world's challenges. So, let us embark on this transformative journey together and discover the power of mindfulness in attaining inner peace.

Mindful Breathing and Meditation Techniques

In today's fast-paced world, finding inner peace seems like an elusive goal. The constant demands of work and personal life can leave us feeling overwhelmed and disconnected from ourselves. However, there is a powerful tool that can help us find balance and attain inner peace – mindful breathing and meditation techniques.

Mindful breathing is a simple yet impactful practice that involves paying attention to our breath. By focusing on our breath, we can anchor ourselves in the present moment and bring our attention away from the chaos and noise of our daily lives. It is a practice that can be done anywhere, anytime, making it accessible to all types of individuals.

To begin, find a comfortable position – whether it's sitting or lying down – and close your eyes. Take a few deep breaths, inhaling through your nose and exhaling through your mouth. As you inhale, feel the coolness of the air entering your nostrils, and as you exhale, notice the warmth leaving your body. Pay attention to the sensation of the breath in your body – the rise and fall of your chest or the expansion and contraction of your abdomen.

As thoughts arise, gently acknowledge them without judgment and bring your focus back to your breath. This practice of mindful breathing can help calm the mind, reduce stress, and increase self-awareness. It allows us to observe our thoughts and emotions without getting caught up in them, fostering a sense of inner peace and clarity.

In addition to mindful breathing, incorporating meditation techniques into your daily routine can further enhance your journey towards inner peace. Meditation involves intentionally setting aside time to sit quietly and focus your attention. There are various meditation techniques to explore, such as loving-kindness meditation, body scan meditation, or guided visualization.

Loving-kindness meditation involves cultivating feelings of love, compassion, and goodwill towards ourselves and others. Body scan meditation involves systematically bringing awareness to different parts of the body, noticing any sensations or tension. Guided visualization involves using your imagination to create a peaceful, calming mental image.

No matter which technique resonates with you, the key is to approach it with an open mind and a willingness to explore. Consistency is also essential –

even just a few minutes of daily practice can yield significant benefits over time.

Balancing work and life for inner peace requires intentional effort and the cultivation of mindfulness. By incorporating mindful breathing and meditation techniques into your routine, you can create a space for yourself to find calm amidst the chaos. Remember, inner peace is not a destination but a journey, and these techniques serve as valuable tools to guide you along the way.

Incorporating Mindfulness into Daily Life

In today's fast-paced and demanding world, finding inner peace and achieving a sense of balance can often feel like an elusive goal. The constant juggling act between work and personal life can leave us feeling overwhelmed, stressed, and disconnected from ourselves. However, by incorporating mindfulness into our daily routines, we can cultivate a greater sense of calm, clarity, and inner peace.

Mindfulness is the practice of being fully present and aware of the present moment, without judgment. It involves paying attention to our thoughts, feelings, and bodily sensations, as well as the world around us. By incorporating mindfulness into our daily lives, we can learn to respond to challenges with greater clarity and compassion, rather than reacting impulsively.

One of the first steps in incorporating mindfulness into daily life is to start with small moments of mindfulness throughout the day. This can be as simple as pausing for a few moments to take a deep breath and tune into our senses. Whether it's savoring a cup of tea, taking a mindful walk during a lunch break, or even just noticing the sensations of our body while washing dishes, these small moments can help anchor us in the present moment and bring a sense of calm.

Another powerful way to incorporate mindfulness into daily life is through the practice of mindful eating. Many of us have developed a habit of mindlessly consuming our meals, often while multitasking or rushing through our day. By taking the time to fully engage with our food, noticing its flavors, textures, and smells, we can bring a greater sense of enjoyment and gratitude into our daily lives.

Mindfulness can also be integrated into our work life, helping us to achieve a better balance between professional responsibilities and personal well-being. Taking short breaks throughout the day to practice mindful breathing or engaging in brief mindfulness exercises can help reduce stress and improve focus and productivity.

Additionally, incorporating mindfulness into our interactions with others can strengthen our relationships and enhance our communication skills. By being fully present and attentive during conversations, we can cultivate deeper connections and understanding with our loved ones, colleagues, and even strangers.

Incorporating mindfulness into daily life is not about adding more to our already busy schedules; it's about finding moments of presence and awareness within the activities we are already engaged in. By making a conscious effort to slow down, tune in, and savor the present moment, we can cultivate a greater sense of balance, inner peace, and well-being in the modern world.

Chapter 6: Developing Self-Care Habits

Importance of Self-Care for Inner Peace: Importance of Self-Care for Inner Peace

In our fast-paced modern world, finding inner peace can often feel like an elusive goal. The demands of work, family, and personal responsibilities can leave us feeling overwhelmed, stressed, and disconnected from ourselves. However, by prioritizing self-care, we can regain balance in our lives and cultivate a sense of inner peace that can positively impact every aspect of our existence.

Self-care is not a luxury; it is a vital necessity for maintaining our physical, mental, and emotional well-being. It encompasses a range of activities and practices that nourish and rejuvenate us on all levels. When we neglect self-care, we risk burnout, chronic stress, and a diminished quality of life. By prioritizing self-care, we give ourselves the opportunity to recharge, replenish our inner resources, and restore a sense of equilibrium.

Balancing work and life is a key aspect of self-care for achieving inner peace. Often, we find ourselves caught in a never-ending cycle of work-related obligations, leaving little time for personal fulfillment and self-care. Recognizing the importance of setting boundaries and creating space for activities that bring us joy is crucial. By carving out time for hobbies, exercise, relaxation, and quality time with loved ones, we can cultivate a sense of balance that promotes inner peace.

Moreover, self-care involves nourishing our physical bodies. Regular exercise, proper nutrition, and adequate sleep are essential for overall well-being and inner peace. Engaging in activities that promote physical health can also have a profound impact on our mental and emotional well-being. When our bodies are healthy and energized, we are better equipped to face the challenges of daily life with a sense of calm and clarity.

In addition to physical self-care, nurturing our mental and emotional states is equally important. Engaging in mindfulness practices such as meditation, deep breathing exercises, and journaling can help quiet the mind and cultivate a sense of inner calm. Seeking support from therapists, coaches, or mentors can also provide valuable guidance and tools for managing stress and enhancing our overall well-being.

Remember, achieving and maintaining inner peace is a lifelong journey that requires consistent effort and self-reflection. By prioritizing self-care, we honor ourselves and create the conditions necessary for inner peace to flourish. So, take a moment today to reflect on your self-care practices and consider how you can prioritize your own well-being. By doing so, you can create a life that is balanced, fulfilling, and filled with inner peace.

Physical Self-Care Practices

In today's fast-paced and demanding world, finding inner peace can often feel like an elusive goal. We often find ourselves struggling to balance our work and personal lives, leaving little time for self-care. However, taking care of our physical well-being is crucial for achieving inner peace. In this subchapter, we will explore various physical self-care practices that can help us attain a mindful balance in the modern world.

Exercise is one of the most effective ways to take care of our bodies and minds. Engaging in regular physical activity not only improves our physical health but also releases endorphins, the feel-good hormones that boost our mood and reduce stress. Whether it's going for a run, practicing yoga, or taking a dance class, finding an exercise routine that suits your preferences and schedule is essential for maintaining a healthy work-life balance.

Another important aspect of physical self-care is nourishing our bodies with nutritious foods. A well-balanced diet provides us with the energy and nutrients we need to function optimally. Incorporating fruits, vegetables, whole grains, and lean proteins into our meals can boost our immune system, improve our focus, and enhance our overall well-being. Moreover, mindful eating practices, such as being present and savoring each bite, can help us reconnect with our bodies and cultivate a sense of inner peace.

In addition to exercise and nutrition, self-care also involves taking care of our physical appearance. It may seem superficial, but looking good can significantly impact our self-confidence and overall happiness. Taking the time to groom ourselves, dress in clothes that make us feel comfortable and confident, and practicing good hygiene can enhance our self-esteem and contribute to a more balanced and peaceful state of mind.

Lastly, getting enough restorative sleep is essential for physical and mental rejuvenation. Lack of sleep can lead to decreased productivity, increased stress levels, and a weakened immune system. By prioritizing a consistent sleep routine, creating a peaceful sleep environment, and practicing relaxation techniques before bedtime, we can improve the quality of our sleep and wake up feeling refreshed and ready to face the day.

conclusion,

physical self-care practices play a vital role in achieving inner peace in the modern world. By incorporating regular exercise, nourishing our bodies with nutritious foods, taking care of our physical appearance, and prioritizing restorative sleep, we can cultivate a mindful balance between work and life. Remember, taking care of ourselves is not selfish but rather a necessary investment in our overall well-being. So, let us embark on this journey of physical self-care and discover the profound impact it can have on our inner peace.

Emotional and Mental Self-Care Practices

In the fast-paced and demanding modern world, finding inner peace and achieving a healthy work-life balance has become increasingly challenging. The constant juggling of responsibilities, deadlines, and expectations can take a toll on our emotional and mental well-being. However, by incorporating mindful and intentional self-care practices into our lives, we can nurture our emotional and mental health, leading to a more balanced and fulfilling existence.

1. Practice Mindfulness: Mindfulness is the art of being fully present in the moment, without judgment. It allows us to observe our thoughts and emotions without getting caught up in them. By incorporating mindfulness into our daily routine, we can cultivate a greater sense of self-awareness, reduce stress, and enhance emotional resilience.

2. Cultivate Gratitude: Gratitude has the power to shift our perspective and bring us back to the present. Take a few moments each day to reflect on the things you are grateful for. This simple practice can help you appreciate the small joys in life, enhance your overall well-being, and foster a positive mindset.

3. Prioritize Self-Care: It is essential to prioritize self-care to maintain a healthy work-life balance. Engage in activities that bring you joy and relaxation, whether it's reading a book, taking a walk in nature, or practicing yoga. Remember, self-care is not selfish; it is necessary for your emotional and mental well-being.

4. Set Boundaries: Establishing clear boundaries between work and personal life is crucial to maintaining inner peace. Learn to say no when necessary and create designated time for rest and rejuvenation. Setting boundaries will help you create a healthier and more sustainable work-life integration.

5. Connect with Others: Human connection is vital for our emotional well-being. Make time to nurture your relationships with loved ones, friends, and colleagues. Engage in meaningful conversations, seek support when needed, and practice active listening. Connection and social support are invaluable resources for maintaining inner peace.

6. Practice Self-Compassion: Treat yourself with kindness and compassion. Acknowledge that it's okay to make mistakes and experience setbacks.

Practice self-compassion by speaking to yourself with the same kindness and understanding you would offer to a dear friend. Embrace self-acceptance and let go of self-judgment.

In the quest for balancing work and life for inner peace, incorporating these emotional and mental self-care practices can make a significant difference. Remember, finding inner peace is a journey, and it requires consistent effort and commitment. By prioritizing self-care, setting boundaries, and cultivating mindfulness, you can attain a mindful balance that allows you to thrive in the modern world. Take the first step today and embark on a transformative journey towards inner peace and well-being.

Chapter 7: Nurturing Relationships for Inner Peace

Balancing Personal and Professional Relationships

In today's fast-paced and demanding world, finding a balance between personal and professional relationships is crucial for our overall well-being and inner peace. The constant juggling act between work and personal life can cause stress, burnout, and strain on our relationships. However, with mindful balance, it is possible to harmonize these two aspects of our lives and cultivate inner peace.

In this subchapter, we will explore strategies and techniques to help you achieve a healthy and fulfilling balance between your personal and professional relationships. These principles apply to all types of individuals, regardless of their occupation or lifestyle. Whether you are a dedicated professional, a stay-at-home parent, an entrepreneur, or someone just starting their career, finding harmony in these areas is essential for your overall happiness and well-being.

We will begin by examining the detrimental effects of an imbalance between personal and professional life. From increased stress levels to strained relationships, we will delve into the consequences of neglecting one aspect of our lives at the expense of the other. Understanding these consequences will serve as a motivation to prioritize balance and make necessary changes in our lives.

Next, we will explore practical strategies and tools to achieve this balance. From setting boundaries and managing time effectively to prioritizing self-care and fostering open communication, we will provide actionable steps that can be implemented in both personal and professional relationships. Additionally, we will discuss the importance of mindfulness in maintaining balance and offer mindfulness exercises to promote self-awareness and emotional well-being.

Furthermore, we will address specific challenges and dilemmas that may arise when balancing personal and professional relationships. Whether it's managing work-life integration, dealing with conflicts between personal and professional commitments, or finding quality time for loved ones, we will provide guidance to navigate these complexities and make conscious choices that promote harmony and inner peace.

Finally, we will highlight inspiring stories and testimonials from individuals who have successfully achieved balance in their personal and professional relationships. These real-life examples will serve as a source of inspiration and motivation, showcasing that it is indeed possible to find harmony amidst the demands of the modern world.

By implementing the strategies and principles outlined in this subchapter, you will be able to cultivate a sense of inner peace, enhance your overall well-being, and build stronger and more fulfilling relationships both personally and professionally. Remember, achieving balance is an ongoing journey, and with mindfulness and conscious effort, you can attain the peace and fulfillment you deserve.

Effective Communication for Harmonious Relationships

In today's fast-paced and interconnected world, it is easy to overlook the importance of effective communication in maintaining harmonious relationships. Whether it is within our personal lives or in the workplace, the ability to communicate effectively plays a pivotal role in fostering understanding, resolving conflicts, and ultimately attaining inner peace.

Effective communication is not just about speaking clearly; it encompasses active listening, empathy, and openness to different perspectives. It is a two-way street that requires effort and mindfulness from all parties involved. It is a skill that can be developed and honed over time, leading to stronger, more fulfilling relationships.

One of the key aspects of effective communication is active listening. It involves giving our full attention to the person speaking, without interrupting or formulating a response in our minds. Active listening allows us to truly understand the other person's thoughts, feelings, and concerns, fostering a sense of empathy and connection.

Empathy is the ability to put ourselves in someone else's shoes and understand their emotions and experiences. It is a powerful tool in fostering harmonious relationships, as it allows us to validate the other person's feelings and respond with compassion and understanding. By practicing empathy, we can create an environment of trust and support, enhancing our relationships and promoting inner peace.

Openness to different perspectives is another crucial aspect of effective communication. It is natural for individuals to have differing viewpoints and opinions, and embracing this diversity can lead to more creative and innovative solutions. By actively seeking out different perspectives and engaging in constructive dialogue, we can bridge gaps in understanding and find common ground, further strengthening our relationships.

Balancing work and life for inner peace is a challenge that many individuals face in the modern world. Effective communication plays a vital role in achieving this balance. By communicating our needs, boundaries, and priorities with clarity and assertiveness, we can foster understanding and support from both our personal and professional circles. This, in turn, enables us to create a harmonious environment where our work and personal lives coexist in a way that brings us inner peace.

conclusion,

effective communication is an essential skill for maintaining harmonious relationships in all aspects of life. By practicing active listening, empathy, and openness to different perspectives, we can foster understanding, resolve conflicts, and attain inner peace. Whether it is in our personal relationships or in the pursuit of balancing work and life, effective communication is the key to nurturing harmonious connections and finding tranquility in the modern world.

Cultivating Empathy and Compassion in Relationships

In today's fast-paced and interconnected world, it's easy to get caught up in the hustle and bustle of daily life and forget about the importance of nurturing our relationships. Whether it's with our partners, family members, friends, or colleagues, cultivating empathy and compassion is key to maintaining healthy and fulfilling connections. In this subchapter, we will explore practical strategies to help you foster empathy and compassion in your relationships, ultimately leading to a greater sense of inner peace.

Empathy, the ability to understand and share the feelings of another person, is the foundation of strong relationships. By putting ourselves in someone else's shoes, we can gain a deeper understanding of their experiences and emotions. To cultivate empathy, start by actively listening to others without judgment. Truly hearing someone's words and paying attention to their body language can help you grasp their perspective.

Compassion, on the other hand, goes beyond understanding and involves a genuine desire to alleviate the suffering of others. It is the driving force behind acts of kindness and support. To cultivate compassion, practice self-compassion first. Treat yourself with kindness and acceptance, acknowledging that you too are deserving of love and understanding. By extending this compassion towards others, you create an environment where empathy and compassion can thrive.

One powerful way to enhance empathy and compassion in relationships is through mindful communication. Mindfulness involves being fully present in the moment, free from distractions and preconceived notions. By practicing mindful communication, you can become more attuned to the needs and emotions of others. Take the time to truly listen, validate their feelings, and respond with empathy and kindness.

Another effective strategy is to practice gratitude. Expressing gratitude towards your loved ones can strengthen your bond and foster a sense of connection. Make it a habit to appreciate and acknowledge the positive aspects of your relationships, both big and small. By cultivating gratitude, you create a positive and nurturing environment that allows empathy and compassion to flourish.

Finally, remember that cultivating empathy and compassion is an ongoing journey. It requires patience, understanding, and a willingness to learn and grow. As you continue to prioritize empathy and compassion in your relationships, you will not only experience greater inner peace but also create a ripple effect that positively impacts those around you.

In conclusion, nurturing empathy and compassion in relationships is essential for achieving a sense of balance and inner peace in our hectic lives. By actively practicing empathy, compassion, mindful communication, and gratitude, we can foster deeper connections and create a more harmonious and fulfilling existence. Let us embark on this journey together, embracing the power of empathy and compassion to transform our relationships and ourselves.

Chapter 8: Embracing Minimalism and Simplifying Your Life

Understanding the Benefits of Minimalism

In our fast-paced, consumer-driven society, the concept of minimalism has gained significant attention as a means to find balance and attain inner peace. Minimalism is not just about decluttering physical spaces; it is a mindset that encourages us to simplify our lives and focus on the things that truly matter. This subchapter aims to shed light on the various benefits of embracing minimalism, providing valuable insights for individuals from all walks of life, especially those seeking to balance work and personal life for inner peace.

One of the primary advantages of minimalism is the sense of freedom it brings. By reducing the number of possessions and commitments, we free up mental and physical space, allowing ourselves to breathe and think more clearly. This newfound freedom enables us to focus on our priorities, be it spending quality time with loved ones, pursuing personal passions, or engaging in self-care practices. Minimalism empowers us to break free from the cycle of mindless consumerism, where material possessions often become a source of stress and distraction.

Moreover, minimalism helps us cultivate a greater sense of gratitude and appreciation for what we have. By intentionally choosing to surround ourselves with only the essentials, we become more aware of the value and significance of each item and experience. This shift in perspective allows us to be more mindful of the present moment, fostering a deeper connection with ourselves and our surroundings.

Minimalism also encourages sustainable and environmentally conscious living. By reducing our consumption and embracing a more minimalist lifestyle, we contribute to the preservation of our planet's resources. By consuming less and choosing quality over quantity, we minimize waste and ecological footprint, leaving a positive impact on future generations.

Additionally, minimalism offers numerous mental health benefits. By decluttering both our physical and mental spaces, we alleviate stress and anxiety, creating a more peaceful and harmonious internal environment. With fewer distractions and a clearer focus, we become more productive and efficient, both in our personal and professional lives. By prioritizing what truly matters to us, we eliminate the overwhelm of juggling multiple responsibilities, allowing us to achieve a healthier work-life balance.

In conclusion, embracing minimalism can have transformative effects on our lives, helping us find inner peace amidst the chaos of the modern world. By simplifying our lives, focusing on what truly matters, and letting go of non-essential distractions, we create space for genuine happiness, fulfillment, and tranquility. Whether you are a busy professional, a parent, or simply someone seeking a more balanced and peaceful existence, minimalism offers invaluable benefits that can positively impact all aspects of your life.

Decluttering and Organizing Your Physical Space

In today's fast-paced world, finding inner peace can often seem like an elusive goal. The constant demands of work and the overwhelming responsibilities of daily life can leave us feeling stressed, anxious, and disconnected from ourselves. However, there is a simple yet powerful practice that can help us achieve a sense of inner calm amidst the chaos: decluttering and organizing our physical space.

Our external environment has a profound impact on our internal state. When our surroundings are chaotic and cluttered, it becomes difficult to focus, think clearly, and find peace within ourselves. On the other hand, a clean, organized space can create a sense of calm and promote a harmonious flow of energy.

Decluttering is the first step towards creating a balanced and peaceful living space. It involves clearing out the physical clutter that accumulates over time, such as excess belongings, old papers, and unnecessary items. By letting go of what no longer serves us, we create space for new possibilities and a fresh start.

Organizing goes hand in hand with decluttering, as it ensures that everything has its place and is easily accessible. Adopting effective organizational systems can save us time, reduce stress, and increase productivity. Whether it's implementing a filing system for important documents, creating designated spaces for different activities, or utilizing storage solutions, finding organizational methods that work for us is crucial for maintaining an organized space in the long run.

The benefits of decluttering and organizing our physical space extend far beyond just tidiness. When we take the time to declutter, we also declutter our minds. Letting go of physical possessions can be a deeply transformative process that teaches us to detach from material attachments and cultivate a sense of gratitude for what truly matters.

Moreover, an organized space can improve our overall well-being. Studies have shown that living in a clutter-free environment can reduce stress levels, enhance focus and concentration, and even improve sleep quality. By creating an environment that supports our well-being, we empower ourselves to live a more balanced and fulfilling life.

Balancing work and life for inner peace requires us to create boundaries and prioritize self-care. Decluttering and organizing our physical space is an essential aspect of this process. By dedicating time and energy to decluttering and organizing, we are actively investing in our own well-being and cultivating a peaceful and balanced life.

In conclusion, decluttering and organizing our physical space is a powerful practice that can help us attain inner peace in the modern world. By letting go of what no longer serves us and creating an organized environment, we create space for clarity, focus, and harmony. Whether it's decluttering our homes or organizing our workspaces, this practice empowers us to live a more balanced and fulfilling life. So, take the first step today and embark on a journey of decluttering and organizing for a more peaceful and mindful existence.

Simplifying Your Digital Life

In today's fast-paced, technology-driven world, it's easy to become overwhelmed by the constant barrage of digital distractions. From emails and social media notifications to endless to-do lists and work-related demands, our digital lives can quickly take over, leaving us feeling stressed and disconnected from ourselves and those around us. However, finding inner peace amidst the chaos is possible, and it begins with simplifying your digital life.

This subchapter aims to guide readers of all types, from busy professionals to stay-at-home parents, on how to navigate the digital landscape in a way that promotes balance and inner peace. By implementing the following strategies, you can regain control over your digital habits and create a more mindful and fulfilling life.

First and foremost, it's crucial to set boundaries. Establish specific times during the day when you will dedicate yourself to digital tasks, such as checking emails or engaging with social media. Outside of these designated periods, make a conscious effort to disconnect and focus on other aspects of your life that bring you joy and fulfillment. By creating clear boundaries, you can prevent technology from dominating your every waking moment.

Next, practice digital decluttering. Just as physical clutter can overwhelm our living spaces, digital clutter can clutter our minds. Take the time to clean up your digital spaces by organizing your emails, deleting unnecessary files, and unsubscribing from newsletters and notifications that no longer serve you. By simplifying your digital environment, you can reduce distractions and create a more serene and focused mindset.

Another important aspect of simplifying your digital life is the practice of mindful technology usage. Rather than mindlessly scrolling through social media or compulsively checking your smartphone, approach your digital interactions with intention and awareness. Ask yourself whether your engagement with technology aligns with your values and priorities. By being mindful of how you use technology, you can ensure that it enhances your life rather than detracts from it.

Finally, embrace the power of unplugging. Regularly disconnecting from technology can have profound benefits for your mental and emotional well-being. Set aside dedicated time each day to engage in activities that don't involve screens, such as going for a walk in nature, practicing mindfulness or meditation, or engaging in hobbies and creative pursuits. By consciously stepping away from the digital world, you can cultivate a sense of inner peace and reestablish a deeper connection with yourself and those around you.

In conclusion, simplifying your digital life is essential for finding inner peace and balance in today's modern world. By setting boundaries, practicing digital decluttering, adopting mindful technology usage, and embracing unplugging, you can regain control over your digital habits and create a more meaningful and fulfilling life. Remember, your digital life should serve you, not the other way around.

Chapter 9: Overcoming Stress and Anxiety

Identifying Sources of Stress and Anxiety

In our fast-paced and demanding modern world, it is no wonder that stress and anxiety have become common experiences for people of all types. Whether you are a working professional, a stay-at-home parent, or a student, finding the balance between work and life can be a challenge. However, understanding the sources of stress and anxiety is the first step towards attaining inner peace.

One of the major sources of stress is the relentless pressure to achieve success in our professional lives. The constant need to meet deadlines, exceed expectations, and compete with others can leave us feeling overwhelmed and exhausted. Additionally, the fear of failure and the uncertainty of job security can contribute to feelings of anxiety. It is crucial to recognize these stressors and find ways to manage them effectively.

Another significant source of stress and anxiety is the imbalance between work and personal life. Many of us find ourselves caught in the never-ending cycle of working long hours, neglecting our relationships, and sacrificing our own well-being. This imbalance can result in feelings of guilt, isolation, and burnout. It is essential to prioritize self-care, set boundaries, and create a healthy work-life balance to reduce stress and promote inner peace.

Furthermore, technological advancements have revolutionized the way we work and communicate, but they have also added new sources of stress and anxiety. The constant connectivity and the expectation of immediate responses can lead to a feeling of being always "on" and never truly able to switch off. It is crucial to recognize the impact of technology on our well-being and establish healthy digital boundaries to protect our mental health.

Additionally, personal relationships, financial worries, health concerns, and societal pressures can all contribute to stress and anxiety. Identifying these sources and understanding their impact on our lives is crucial for our overall well-being and inner peace.

In this subchapter, we will explore various techniques and strategies to help identify the sources of stress and anxiety in your life. We will delve into self-reflection exercises, mindfulness practices, and stress management techniques that can empower you to regain control and find balance. By acknowledging and addressing the sources of stress and anxiety, you can take steps towards attaining inner peace and living a more fulfilling life.

Remember, you are not alone in this journey. By understanding the common sources of stress and anxiety, and implementing the strategies outlined in this subchapter, you can find the balance you seek and attain inner peace in the modern world.

Stress Management Techniques

In today's fast-paced world, finding inner peace can seem like a daunting task. Our lives have become increasingly filled with responsibilities, deadlines, and the constant pressure to achieve more. It's no wonder that stress has become a common companion for many of us. However, there are effective techniques that can help us manage and reduce stress, allowing us to attain inner peace amidst the hustle and bustle of our modern lives.

One of the most essential stress management techniques is practicing mindfulness. Mindfulness is the art of being fully present in the moment, without judgment. By tuning into our thoughts, emotions, and physical sensations, we can gain a deeper understanding of ourselves and our reactions to stressors. Mindfulness can be cultivated through various practices such as meditation, deep breathing exercises, or simply taking a few minutes each day to focus on the present moment.

Another technique for balancing work and life for inner peace is setting boundaries. Often, stress arises from feeling overwhelmed by the demands of work and personal life blurring together. By setting clear boundaries between these two areas, we can create a sense of structure and prioritize our well-being. This may involve creating a dedicated workspace, scheduling regular breaks, and learning to say no when necessary. Setting boundaries allows us to maintain a healthy work-life balance and prevent stress from seeping into every aspect of our lives.

Additionally, engaging in regular physical exercise is an effective way to manage stress. Exercise releases endorphins, which are natural mood enhancers, and helps to reduce tension in the body. Whether it's going for a run, practicing yoga, or participating in a team sport, finding a form of exercise that resonates with you can greatly contribute to your overall well-being and inner peace.

Lastly, seeking support from others can provide significant relief from stress. Surrounding yourself with a supportive network of friends, family, or even joining a stress management group can offer a sense of belonging and understanding. Sharing your thoughts and feelings with others who may be going through similar challenges can provide valuable insights and strategies for coping with stress.

conclusion,

finding inner peace in the modern world requires conscious effort and the application of stress management techniques. By practicing mindfulness, setting boundaries, engaging in regular exercise, and seeking support, we can navigate the challenges of balancing work and life, reduce stress, and attain inner peace. Remember, it's important to prioritize self-care and make room for activities that bring joy and relaxation into our lives.

Coping Strategies for Dealing with Anxiety

Introduction:
In today's fast-paced world, anxiety has become a prevalent issue for people from all walks of life. Whether you are a working professional, a stay-at-home parent, or a student, finding balance and inner peace can sometimes feel like an overwhelming challenge. However, by implementing coping strategies specifically designed to address anxiety, you can reclaim control over your thoughts and emotions and achieve a state of mindful balance. In this subchapter, we will explore effective coping strategies that can help you navigate the turbulent waters of anxiety and attain inner peace.

Understanding Anxiety:
Before we delve into coping strategies, it is crucial to understand anxiety and its impact on our lives. Anxiety is a natural response to stress and can manifest as feelings of unease, worry, or fear. When left unmanaged, anxiety can significantly hinder our ability to find balance and inner peace, affecting both our personal and professional lives.

Coping Strategies:
1. Mindfulness Meditation: One of the most powerful tools for managing anxiety is mindfulness meditation. By focusing your attention on the present moment and observing your thoughts without judgment, you can cultivate a sense of calm and detachment from anxious thoughts and emotions.

2. Breathing Techniques: Deep breathing exercises can help regulate your nervous system and reduce anxiety. Try diaphragmatic breathing, where you inhale deeply through your nose, filling your belly, and exhale slowly through your mouth. This simple technique can instantly calm your mind and body.

3. Physical Exercise: Engaging in regular physical activity releases endorphins, which elevate mood and reduce stress. Incorporate activities such as yoga, jogging, or dancing into your routine to help manage anxiety and promote inner peace.

4. Self-Care: Prioritize self-care to nourish your mind and body. Establish a routine that includes activities you enjoy, such as reading, taking relaxing baths, or spending time in nature. By taking care of yourself, you can build resilience and better cope with anxiety.

5. Seek Support: Do not hesitate to reach out for support when needed. Whether it's confiding in a trusted friend or seeking professional help, sharing your anxieties can offer relief and provide guidance on managing anxiety effectively.

Conclusion:

Anxiety may be a common struggle, but it doesn't have to control your life. By implementing these coping strategies, you can regain control over your thoughts and emotions, finding the balance needed to achieve inner peace. Remember, it's essential to be patient with yourself as you navigate this journey. With practice and perseverance, you can overcome anxiety and cultivate a sense of mindful balance in the modern world.

Chapter 10: Maintaining Balance in a Fast-Paced World

Strategies for Staying Grounded Amidst Chaos

In today's fast-paced world, finding inner peace can seem like an impossible task. The constant demands of work and personal life can leave us feeling overwhelmed and disconnected from ourselves. However, it is crucial to remember that amidst the chaos, we have the power to cultivate a sense of inner calm and balance. In this subchapter of "Mindful Balance: Attaining Inner Peace in the Modern World," we explore various strategies to help you stay grounded amidst the chaos and find inner peace.

1. Practice Mindfulness: Mindfulness is the practice of being fully present in the moment, without judgment. By cultivating mindfulness, we can learn to observe our thoughts and emotions without getting caught up in them. Incorporate mindfulness into your daily routine by taking a few minutes each day to engage in activities such as meditation, deep breathing, or simply being aware of your surroundings.

2. Set Boundaries: Balancing work and life is essential for maintaining inner peace. Learn to set boundaries and prioritize your well-being. Make time for self-care activities, such as exercise, hobbies, and spending quality time with loved ones. Remember, saying "no" to certain commitments is not a sign of weakness but rather a way of respecting your own needs.

3. Embrace Imperfection: Often, we strive for perfection in all aspects of our lives, which only adds to our stress and anxiety. Instead, embrace imperfection and practice self-compassion. Understand that it is okay to make mistakes and that they are opportunities for growth. Be kind to yourself and celebrate your accomplishments, no matter how small.

4. Disconnect from Technology: In today's digital age, it is easy to become constantly connected and overwhelmed by notifications and information overload. Take regular breaks from technology to disconnect and recharge. Engage in activities that promote relaxation and rejuvenation, such as reading, spending time in nature, or practicing a hobby.

5. Cultivate Gratitude: Amidst chaos, it is essential to find moments of gratitude. Take time each day to reflect on the things you are grateful for,

whether it be the support of loved ones, the beauty of nature, or your own personal strengths. Cultivating gratitude can shift your perspective and help you find peace amidst the chaos.

Remember, finding inner peace is an ongoing journey that requires consistent effort and self-reflection. By incorporating these strategies into your life, you can create a sense of balance and find inner peace even amidst the chaos of the modern world. Take small steps each day and be patient with yourself. You deserve to live a life filled with inner peace and harmony.

Creating a Sustainable Routine for Inner Peace

In today's fast-paced and hectic world, finding inner peace can feel like an elusive goal. Balancing work and life can often leave us feeling overwhelmed, stressed, and disconnected from ourselves. However, by establishing a sustainable routine that promotes inner peace, we can navigate the challenges of modern life with greater ease and tranquility.

The key to creating a sustainable routine for inner peace is to cultivate mindfulness and balance in all aspects of our lives. This subchapter explores practical strategies and actionable tips that can be applied by all types of individuals, regardless of their specific circumstances or backgrounds.

One of the first steps towards establishing a sustainable routine is to prioritize self-care. Taking care of our physical, emotional, and mental well-being is crucial for maintaining inner peace. This may involve incorporating activities such as exercise, meditation, journaling, or engaging in hobbies that bring joy and relaxation. By dedicating time to recharge and nurture ourselves, we can approach our daily responsibilities with renewed energy and a calmer mindset.

Another important aspect of creating a sustainable routine is setting boundaries and managing our time effectively. Balancing work and life is essential for attaining inner peace. It is crucial to establish clear boundaries between work and personal life, ensuring that we create time for rest, relationships, and activities that bring us fulfillment. By prioritizing our well-being and setting realistic expectations, we can avoid burnout and maintain a harmonious work-life balance.

In addition, incorporating mindfulness practices into our routine can significantly enhance our inner peace. Mindfulness involves being fully present in the current moment, without judgment. By practicing mindfulness through techniques such as deep breathing, mindful eating, or simply taking a few minutes to observe our surroundings, we can cultivate a sense of calm and clarity amidst the chaos of daily life.

Creating a sustainable routine for inner peace requires commitment and consistency. It is essential to approach this process with patience and self-compassion, recognizing that it is a journey rather than a destination. As we integrate these practices into our lives, we will gradually experience a greater sense of peace, harmony, and fulfillment. By prioritizing self-care, setting boundaries, and cultivating mindfulness, we can attain inner peace in the modern world, regardless of our unique circumstances.

In conclusion, the path to inner peace is within reach for all types of individuals. By prioritizing self-care, balancing work and life, and incorporating mindfulness practices into our routine, we can create a sustainable foundation for inner peace. Let this subchapter be your guide as you embark on this transformative journey toward attaining inner peace in the modern world. Remember, peace begins within, and it is up to each of us to nurture and cultivate it in our daily lives.

Embracing Flexibility and Adaptability

In today's fast-paced and ever-changing world, it is essential to cultivate flexibility and adaptability in order to achieve inner peace and balance in our lives. The ability to adapt to new situations and be flexible in our thinking allows us to navigate the challenges and demands of work and life more effectively. This subchapter explores the importance of embracing flexibility and adaptability as key tools for finding inner peace in the modern world.

Flexibility is the willingness to change and adjust our plans or perspectives when necessary. It enables us to maintain a sense of balance when unexpected circumstances arise. By embracing flexibility, we can better manage the competing demands of work and personal life. Rather than becoming overwhelmed by rigid schedules and expectations, we can adapt and find creative solutions to achieve a harmonious balance.

Adaptability, on the other hand, is the capacity to adjust and thrive in new or unfamiliar environments. It involves being open-minded and willing to learn from experiences. By embracing adaptability, we can overcome resistance to change and embrace new opportunities for personal and professional growth. This mindset allows us to navigate the complexities of work and life with greater ease and resilience.

Finding inner peace amidst the demands of work and life requires us to cultivate these qualities of flexibility and adaptability. It starts with recognizing that change is inevitable and that we have the power to respond to it in a positive and constructive way. By letting go of fixed expectations and embracing the unknown, we open ourselves up to new possibilities and experiences.

Through mindfulness practices such as meditation and self-reflection, we can develop a deeper awareness of our thoughts, emotions, and reactions. This heightened self-awareness allows us to recognize when we are being rigid or resistant to change. By consciously choosing to be flexible and adaptable, we can release attachments to outcomes and embrace the present moment with acceptance and non-judgment.

In conclusion, embracing flexibility and adaptability is crucial for achieving inner peace in the modern world. By cultivating these qualities, we can navigate the complexities of work and life with greater ease and resilience. Through mindfulness practices and a willingness to let go of fixed expectations, we can embrace change and find balance in the midst of uncertainty. May this subchapter inspire all types of individuals to embark on the path of flexibility and adaptability as a means to attaining inner peace and harmony in their lives.

Chapter 11: Sustaining Inner Peace for Long-term Happiness

Cultivating Gratitude and Positive Thinking

In today's fast-paced and demanding world, finding inner peace can seem like an elusive goal. However, by cultivating gratitude and positive thinking, we can achieve a state of mindful balance and attain the much-needed inner peace we all seek. This subchapter aims to provide practical tools and guidance for people from all walks of life, including those striving to balance work and life for inner peace.

Gratitude is a powerful practice that can transform our perspective on life. By acknowledging and appreciating the blessings, big and small, we can shift our focus from what is lacking to what we already have. In this subchapter, we will explore various exercises and techniques to cultivate gratitude, such as keeping a gratitude journal, expressing thanks to others, and finding beauty in the present moment. By integrating gratitude into our daily lives, we can rewire our brains to notice the positive aspects of life and develop a more optimistic outlook.

Positive thinking goes hand in hand with gratitude, as it involves consciously choosing uplifting thoughts and focusing on what is going well in our lives. This subchapter will delve into the power of positive affirmations and visualization techniques, which can help reprogram our subconscious mind and attract positivity into our lives. We will also explore the impact of surrounding ourselves with positive influences, whether through uplifting books, inspiring mentors, or supportive communities.

For those struggling to balance work and life, this subchapter will offer valuable insights and strategies. We will discuss the importance of setting boundaries, prioritizing self-care, and creating a harmonious work-life integration. By adopting a mindful approach to work and life, we can avoid burnout, reduce stress, and nurture our overall well-being.

Regardless of our circumstances or life situations, cultivating gratitude and positive thinking is a journey that anyone can embark on. By practicing gratitude and embracing positive thoughts, we can transform our lives and find the inner peace we all crave. This subchapter aims to provide practical tools, exercises, and inspiration to support individuals from all backgrounds in their pursuit of mindful balance and attaining inner peace in the modern world.

So, whether you are a busy professional striving to find harmony between work and life or someone seeking solace from the chaos of the modern world, the practices and insights shared in this subchapter will guide you toward a state of mindful balance, gratitude, and positive thinking. Start your journey today and unlock the transformative power of cultivating gratitude and positive thinking for a life filled with inner peace.

Self-Reflection and Continuous Growth

In the pursuit of inner peace, self-reflection, and continuous growth are essential practices that can help us navigate the complexities of modern life. In this subchapter, we delve into the significance of self-reflection and how it contributes to finding the balance between work and life, ultimately leading to inner peace.

Self-reflection allows us to pause and take a step back from the fast-paced world we inhabit. It is a process of introspection, where we examine our thoughts, emotions, and actions with a non-judgmental attitude. By consciously reflecting on our experiences, we gain valuable insights into ourselves and the patterns that influence our lives.

When it comes to balancing work and life, self-reflection becomes even more crucial. Many of us find ourselves caught up in the demands of our careers, often neglecting our personal lives and well-being. By taking the time for self-reflection, we can identify the areas that require attention and make necessary adjustments to achieve a healthier and more fulfilling work-life balance.

Through self-reflection, we can gain clarity on our priorities and values. We can question whether our current choices align with what truly matters to us. This process helps us identify areas where we might be overextending ourselves and neglecting our own needs. By recognizing these imbalances, we can take proactive steps to create a more harmonious and peaceful existence.

Moreover, self-reflection also fosters continuous growth. When we honestly assess ourselves, we become aware of our strengths and weaknesses. This awareness empowers us to work on improving ourselves and developing new skills. By embracing a growth mindset, we cultivate resilience and adaptability, which are essential qualities for finding balance in the ever-changing landscape of work and life.

Self-reflection is not a one-time exercise, but rather an ongoing practice. It requires commitment and a willingness to confront our own vulnerabilities. However, the rewards of self-reflection are immeasurable. It allows us to make conscious choices, prioritize what truly matters, and create a life that aligns with our innermost desires.

In conclusion, self-reflection and continuous growth are integral to achieving inner peace in the modern world. By engaging in self-reflection, we gain valuable insights into ourselves and our lives, enabling us to find the balance between work and life. This process of introspection empowers us to make conscious choices and develop the necessary skills to navigate the complexities of our fast-paced society. By embracing self-reflection as a lifelong practice, we can attain a state of mindful balance and live a more peaceful and fulfilling life.

Building a Supportive Community for Lasting Inner Peace

In today's fast-paced and demanding world, finding inner peace can often feel like an elusive goal. The constant juggling of work and personal life can leave us feeling overwhelmed, stressed, and disconnected from ourselves. However, by building a supportive community, we can create the foundation for lasting inner peace.

A supportive community is a network of individuals who understand the importance of balance and share a common goal of attaining inner peace. It can consist of friends, family, colleagues, or even like-minded individuals whom we meet through various social or professional networks. The key is to surround ourselves with people who uplift us, inspire us, and help us maintain a sense of equilibrium in our lives.

One of the most significant benefits of building a supportive community is the opportunity to share experiences and learn from one another. By engaging in open and honest conversations, we can gain valuable insights into how others navigate the challenges of balancing work and life for inner peace. We can exchange tips, strategies, and techniques that have worked for each of us, helping us discover new ways to harmonize our responsibilities and personal well-being.

Moreover, a supportive community provides a safe space for vulnerability and emotional support. When we face inevitable setbacks or feel overwhelmed, having a network of individuals who understand and empathize with our struggles can be tremendously comforting. They can offer guidance, encouragement, and a listening ear, reminding us that we are not alone in our journey towards inner peace.

Building a supportive community also involves actively contributing to the well-being of others. By offering our support, kindness, and understanding, we create a reciprocal environment where everyone benefits. Acts of generosity and compassion not only help others find their own inner peace but also reinforce our commitment to maintaining a harmonious balance in our own lives.

In conclusion, building a supportive community is essential for attaining lasting inner peace in the modern world. By surrounding ourselves with like-minded individuals who understand the challenges of balancing work and life, we can share experiences, gain insights, and receive emotional support.

Together, we can navigate the complexities of our lives, find solace in connection, and cultivate a sense of inner peace that will endure amidst the chaos of the world. Remember, creating a supportive community is a two-way street, and by offering our support to others, we reinforce our commitment to our own well-being.

Conclusion: Embracing Mindful Balance in the Modern World

In today's fast-paced and chaotic world, finding inner peace may seem like an elusive dream. We are constantly bombarded with never-ending to-do lists, work pressures, and the demands of our personal lives. However, achieving a sense of balance between work and life is not only possible but also essential for our overall well-being. In this subchapter, we will explore the transformative power of embracing mindful balance and how it can help us attain inner peace in the modern world.

Mindful balance is the art of consciously and intentionally allocating our time and energy between work and personal life. It is about recognizing the importance of both aspects and finding a harmonious integration between the two. This concept holds immense potential for all types of individuals, regardless of their profession or lifestyle.

For those struggling to balance work and life, mindful balance offers a practical framework to create a more harmonious existence. By adopting mindful practices such as meditation, self-reflection, and setting boundaries, we can cultivate a greater sense of self-awareness and prioritize what truly matters to us. It enables us to make deliberate choices, ensuring that our time and energy are directed towards activities that nourish our soul and bring us joy.

For professionals seeking inner peace, mindful balance provides a roadmap to overcome burnout and achieve sustainable success. By incorporating mindfulness into our work routines, we can develop a heightened sense of focus, creativity, and resilience. This, in turn, leads to increased productivity, improved decision-making, and enhanced overall well-being.

Moreover, mindful balance extends beyond the individual level and has the potential to positively impact society as a whole. By prioritizing our well-being and finding balance, we become better equipped to contribute to our communities and create positive change. It is through our own inner peace that we can inspire others to embark on their own journey towards mindful balance.

In conclusion, embracing mindful balance in the modern world is not only crucial for our individual well-being but also for creating a more harmonious and peaceful society. By consciously allocating our time and energy between work and personal life, we can achieve a sense of inner peace that transcends the chaos of the external world. The journey towards mindful balance may not always be easy, but its rewards are immeasurable. So, let us take a step back, breathe, and embrace the transformative power of mindful balance.